# the café cookbook

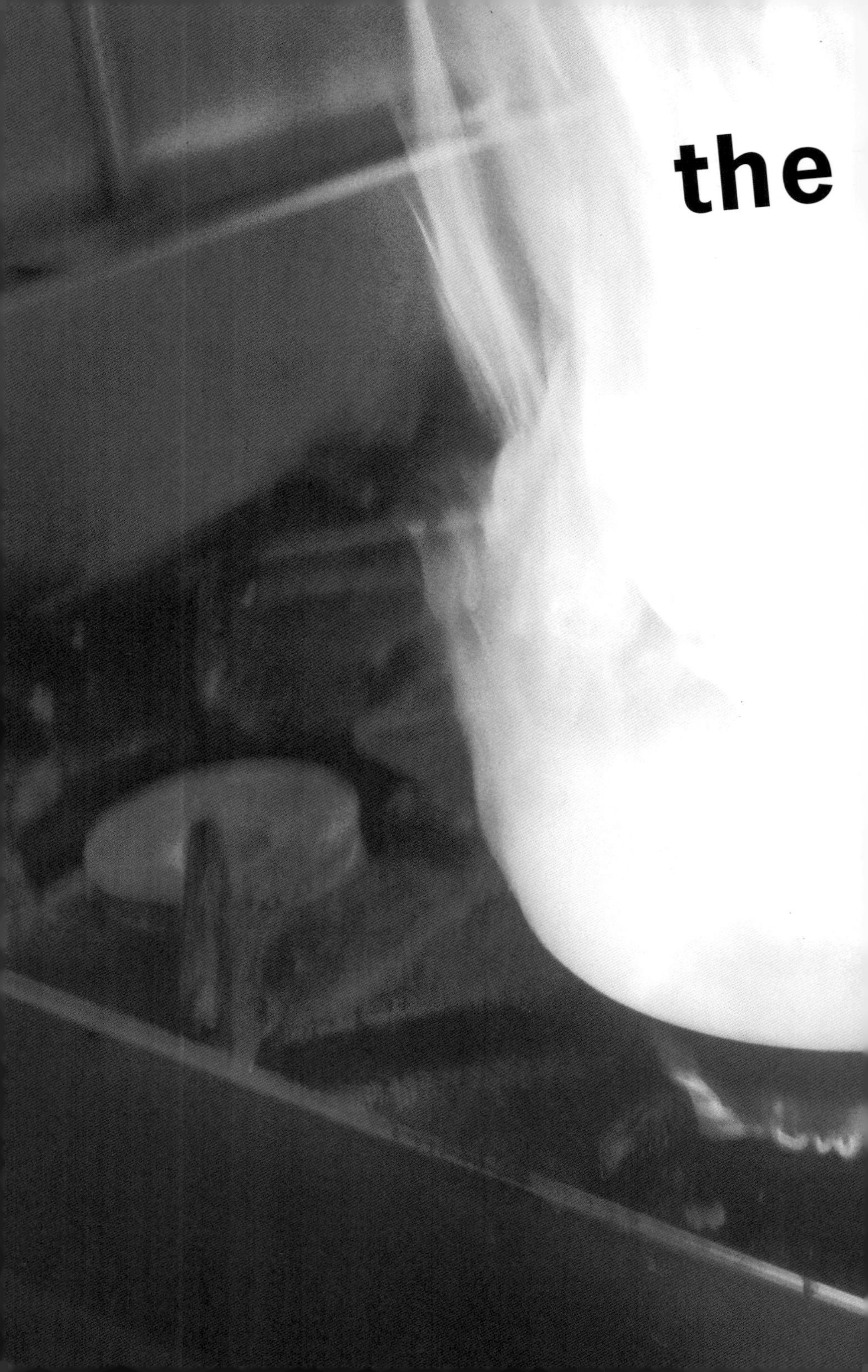
the

# café cookbook

Dianne Taylor

GREAT EATING FROM NEW ZEALAND'S BEST CAFÉS

# ONTENTS

# **A**CKNOWLEDGEMENTS

Our thanks to the proprietors and chefs of the cafes included in this book, in particular Jillene Slui, Anatole's Cafe; Annie Taylor, Andiamo; Luke Macann, Ryan Cole and Douglas Begg, Boat Shed Cafe; Debbie Dornbusch, Cafe Paradiso and City Bistro and Bar; Jennifer McLaughlin, Coyote Street Bar and Restaurant; Julie Le Clerc, The Garnet Road Foodstore; Didier Horand, The Lido Cafe; Kerry Mackay, Mondo Cucina; Sue Leckie, Ombrellos Caffè; Nicky and Tony Smith, Piccolo's Restaurant; Clare Hindmarsh, Safran Cafe Restaurant and Bar; John Redwood, Solera Vino; Esther Lamb, Stella; Bill Bryce, Sumner's Wine Bar and Restaurant; Michael Lucas and Frankie Wee Kok Pau, Zing Cafe.

Thanks, too, to the photographers: David Lowe, Bill Nichol, Lloyd Park, Grant Sheehan, Chris Stills and Sally Tagg.

And to Ngaire Taylor, who would never *ever* boil the veges dry these days!

# **I**NTRODUCTION

**I**t is probably twenty years since the night the carrots boiled dry but I recall the smell vividly; a pervading sickly sweetness mixed with the unmistakable acrid pong of burnt saucepan handle. It was a smell that lingered – temporarily in the house, permanently in my olfactory memory. Someone had forgotten to turn the vegetables down. **M**um taught the piano and it was her habit, between pupils, to set the vegetables to boil at 5 pm. Some time during the next half-hour lesson she would usually remember to nip out and turn them down or at least to yell out to ask one of us kids to. Usually. Sometimes a particularly difficult scale would cause the vegetables to be forgotten until Dad came home from work and turned them down to simmer for another 30 minutes.     **V**egetables were made of tougher stuff back then. Apparently it was necessary to boil them upwards of 40 minutes until they limped, defeated, from the pot onto the plate. There were always three veg, including potato – it wasn't a real meal unless there was potato.     **M**y grandmother was also a piano teacher and it is possible that the ritual turning down of the vegetables was the closest our family ever came to a passed-down culinary tradition. Special occasions aside, our weekly menu was fairly predictable and largely indistinguishable from meals served up and down the country, many of which could probably be traced back to the *Edmonds Cookbook*:

*Monday:*  Leftover topside roast re-heated in leftover gravy, or made into rissoles and three veg
*Tuesday:*  Mince boiled with carrot, celery and peas, thickened with flour, or curried sausages and three veg
*Wednesday:*  Fried chops or wiener schnitzel, Watties tomato sauce and three veg
*Thursday:*  Fried steak, Watties tomato sauce and three veg
*Friday:*  Sweet and sour fish and rice or smoked fish kedgeree (not a 'proper' meal due to the absence of potato!)
*Saturday:*  Roast topside and three veg
*Sunday:*  Scrambled eggs or curried eggs or macaroni cheese or takeaways.

**I**t was not until I travelled to Australia at 19 and ate spaghetti bolognaise at a friend's house that I realised that minced beef could be fried rather than boiled. This discovery was typical of the culinary awakening that so many New Zealanders experienced when they travelled overseas in the years following the late 1960s. When they returned home from Europe and Asia they wouldn't settle any longer for soggy Shrimp Cocktail or Chicken in a Basket. The first wave of the New Zealand culinary revolution had begun.     **T**oday, lifestyle

surveys show that 'eating out' has become a national pastime that is right up there alongside sport, gardening, and reading.    There is no doubt that the explosion of restaurants and cafes around the country has had a major impact on the food we cook at home. While in some homes this simply means that spaghetti bolognaise has replaced macaroni cheese, in others it has translated into pantries and refrigerators stocked with the new staples; pesto, olive oil, sundried tomatoes, goat's cheese, olives, anchovies, curry pastes, coconut cream, chillies, balsamic vinegar, arborio rice, couscous, polenta and fresh pasta. Dried herbs are out, fresh coriander and basil are in. We no longer feel foolish asking the greengrocer for rocket or bok choy.    Ironically, the very fact that New Zealand had no particular cuisine (roast kumara, pipi fritters and pavlova aside) has made us more open to an incredible range of flavours and influences from around the world. Food-conscious New Zealanders are likely to cook Thai food one night, Turkish the next and, while there's certainly a place for authenticity, there's no compulsion to stick strictly to the rules. The most exciting food happening in New Zealand's restaurants today isn't authentic, it's innovative. Our chefs now have the confidence and the skill to break the rules by taking Thai, French, Italian, Vietnamese, Turkish, Japanese and Indian influences, adapting them, and then giving them a final twist.    In more and more homes interesting food is no longer reserved for special occasions, it's on the table every night. That doesn't mean that people are spending longer toiling over a hot stove: quite the opposite. With less time to cook they're turning to simple no-fuss dishes, putting the emphasis on fresh, top-quality ingredients and paying more attention to presentation. Of course it's still fun to occasionally set aside a day and really cook up a storm; home-made stocks and pastas, for example, are well worth the extra effort, but fussy pretentious dinner parties are out. Guests are more likely to be impressed by simple tasty food that hasn't been laboured over.    The recipes in this book are those that can be made easily at home by people who enjoy good food without fuss. Many of them are ideal for cooks who like to walk through the door at 5.30 pm on a week night and be able to place a great meal in front of dinner guests a short time later. Others require a little more time and assume a greater level of skill, but none are overly difficult for good home cooks who are grounded in the basics.    Perhaps the measure of a great cook is the ability to adapt, improvise and innovate. To that end many of the recipes here will serve as starting points for your own ideas. Stick to the recipe the first time, then use your own imagination, fresh seasonal produce, and whatever else happens to be on hand. Remember – life's too short to eat boiled mince! Happy cooking.

*Dianne Taylor*

# Grilled Field Mushrooms with Polenta and Blue Cheese Sauce

**POLENTA**

**1 litre water, well salted**

**300 g polenta**

**olive oil**

**MUSHROOMS**

**2 medium field mushrooms per person**

**olive oil**

**salt and ground pepper**

**SAUCE**

**100 g Kikorangi Blue cheese**

**100 ml cream**

**50 ml white wine**

**1 teaspoon chopped rosemary**

**SALAD**

**rocket leaves**

MAKING THE POLENTA: Bring salted water to the boil and stir in polenta in a slow, steady stream. Simmer gently and stir constantly with a wooden spoon for 25–35 minutes. (Herbs and seasonings can be added to taste.)

When polenta thickens to a smooth porridge pour mixture into a baking dish and leave to set.

When set, turn polenta cake out and portion into wedges. Fry in a little olive oil.

COOKING THE MUSHROOMS: Brush mushrooms with a little olive oil, season and grill at medium temperature.

MAKING THE SAUCE: Crumble cheese into a saucepan with cream and wine. Warm over moderate heat until cheese melts into cream. Add rosemary and reduce to a creamy consistency.

Place polenta wedges and mushrooms on a plate. Coat lightly with sauce. Serve with salad of rocket leaves.

**Serves 4–6**

# Venison on Kumara Mash with Capsicum Marmalade

**VENISON**

**olive oil**

**200 g portion denver leg venison per person**

**¼ cup beef jus (or ready-made beef stock)**

**a little red wine**

**KUMARA MASH**

**golden kumara (enough for 4–6 portions)**

**butter**

**cream**

**freshly ground nutmeg**

**salt and pepper to taste**

**CAPSICUM MARMALADE**

**250 ml water**

**1½ cups sugar**

**¼ cup white vinegar**

**juice and zest of 1 lemon**

**1 apple, peeled, cored and diced**

**4 red capsicums, sliced**

**2 onions, sliced**

**2 whole cloves**

COOKING THE VENISON: Heat a little olive oil in large ovenproof frypan. Sauté venison portions, turning until thoroughly browned, then roast for 8–10 minutes at 250°C. Remove from oven and keep warm.

MAKING THE KUMARA MASH: Wash and peel kumaras. Boil until tender, drain and return to the saucepan over low heat. Add a generous knob of butter and a little cream. Mash. Add nutmeg and seasoning.

MAKING THE MARMALADE: Bring water, sugar, vinegar, lemon juice and zest to the boil. Add apple, capsicums, onions and cloves. Simmer until vegetables are tender and liquid is syrupy. Refrigerate in an airtight jar.

De-glaze the frypan with a little red wine and beef jus.

Slice and arrange venison next to kumara mash on a plate. Dress with pan juices and a tablespoon of marmalade.

**Serves 4–6**

# Cappuccino Ice-Cream Cakes

**ICE-CREAM**

1.5 litres cream

1½ cups caster sugar

6 egg yolks

4 tablespoons ground coffee

2 teaspoons cocoa powder

2 teaspoons Kahlua

**BISCUITS**

2¼ cups rolled oats

1¾ cups caster sugar

3 tablespoons flour

1 tablespoon baking powder

225 g unsalted butter, melted

3 eggs, lightly beaten

**CHOCOLATE SAUCE**

250 g dark chocolate

400–500 ml cream

MAKING THE ICE-CREAM:
Whip cream in a large bowl until lightly peaking. Gradually beat in half the caster sugar by hand.

In another bowl beat egg yolks with remaining sugar until well combined (1–2 minutes). Add coffee, cocoa and Kahlua to egg mix, stirring until all ingredients are well mixed.

Fold egg mixture into cream. Be careful not to over-beat or the mixture will be too stiff.

Pour the mixture into a container, cover and freeze for 4–8 hours. This ice-cream does not need to be stirred during freezing.

MAKING THE BISCUITS: Pre-heat oven to 180°C and grease baking trays. In a large bowl combine rolled oats, caster sugar, flour and baking powder. Stir in melted butter and mix well. Add eggs and mix well.

Spoon dessertspoonsful of mixture onto baking trays, 4 biscuits to each tray. Do not spread mixture and keep biscuits well apart as size will double during baking.

Bake for 5–10 minutes until golden brown. Watch very carefully to avoid burning. When cooked remove from baking tray immediately and cool on a wire rack. Store leftover biscuits in an airtight container.

MAKING THE SAUCE: Combine dark chocolate and cream in a saucepan.

On each plate place a biscuit and top with a scoop of ice-cream. Repeat with another biscuit, top with another scoop of ice-cream and finish with another biscuit. Drizzle chocolate sauce over and serve.

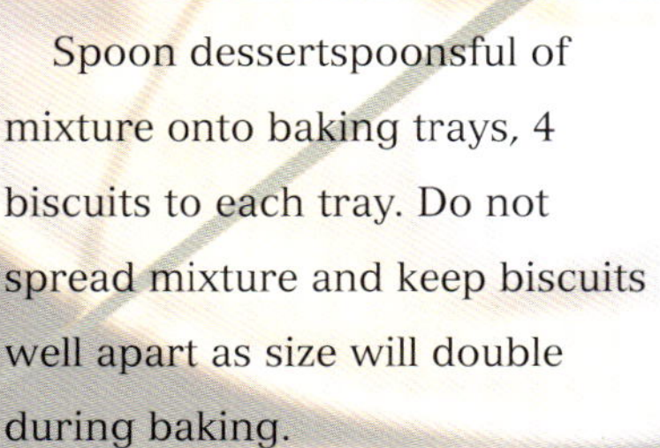

**Serves 8–10**

## Balsamic Beef Salad

**BEEF**

**750 g rare roasted eye fillet of beef, very thinly sliced**

**DRESSING**

**½ cup balsamic vinegar**

**1 cup good-quality olive oil**

**4 cloves garlic, crushed**

**1 teaspoon ground pepper**

**1 teaspoon salt**

**1 teaspoon brown sugar**

**1 teaspoon wholegrain mustard**

**2 tablespoons capers**

**SALAD**

**3 handfuls mesclun (mixed baby salad leaves)**

**½ bunch celery, thinly sliced on a sharp angle**

**1 bunch spring onions, thinly sliced on a sharp angle**

**1 punnet snow pea sprouts**

**caperberries**

COOKING THE BEEF: Sear beef fillet very quickly in a hot frypan to seal juices then roast at 250°C for 30 minutes. Allow to cool.

MAKING THE DRESSING: Whisk together all dressing ingredients except capers. Toss sliced beef in the dressing and allow to marinate for at least 1 hour.

MAKING THE SALAD: Toss salad ingredients, beef and balsamic dressing together well.

Arrange on serving platter and garnish with caperberries.

**Serves 4 as a main, 8 as an entrée**

# Roasted Tomato and Caper Tarte Tatin

**2 red onions, thinly sliced**

**½ cup olive oil**

**12 medium tomatoes, sliced**
**in half**

**salt and ground pepper**

**2 tablespoons balsamic vinegar**

**¼ cup water**

**½ cup sugar**

**2 tablespoons capers**

**300 g puff pastry**

Sweat onions in a little olive oil until softened. Set aside to cool.

Place tomatoes cut-side up in a roasting dish with remaining olive oil. Season. Roast at 180°C for about 1 hour. Cool.

Combine vinegar, water and sugar in a saucepan and boil until a light caramel consistency. Pour into a 28 cm spring-form cake tin lined with non-stick baking paper.

Scatter capers over caramel. Arrange roasted tomatoes, cut-side down, over capers. Cover with cooked onions.

Roll out puff pastry to slightly larger than the cake tin to allow for shrinkage. Place pastry over tomatoes, onions and capers.

Bake at 180°C for 20–30 minutes. Invert onto a serving plate and remove baking paper while still hot so that the caramel doesn't stick.

**Serves 6**

# Espresso and Chocolate Bread-and-Butter Pudding Cake

**200 g butter, softened**

**1 loaf of sliced white sandwich bread (or french bread, sliced)**

**200 g dark chocolate, broken into chunks**

**½ cup sultanas**

**10 eggs**

**½ cup sugar**

**600 ml cream**

**200 ml milk**

**1 teaspoon ground espresso coffee beans**

**100 ml very strong espresso coffee**

**melted chocolate**

**cream**

Butter bread and layer in a 25 cm spring-form cake tin, alternating with chocolate chunks and sultanas. Press down well. Make sure top layer of bread is attractively arranged.

Beat eggs, sugar, cream, milk, ground coffee and espresso coffee together. Pour this mixture gently over the cake until completely absorbed.

Leave for 1 hour until bread swells with the liquid. Bake at 150°C for about 1–1¼ hours. Allow to cool.

When cold, drizzle cake with melted chocolate and dust with icing sugar. Slice and serve with cream.

**Serves 10**

# Gazpacho with Chilli Prawns

**GAZPACHO**

**75 ml red wine vinegar**

**300 ml water**

**1 cucumber, peeled and diced**

**1 red capsicum, de-seeded and finely chopped**

**1 green capsicum, de-seeded and finely chopped**

**1 x 400 g tin whole tomatoes**

**2 cloves garlic, chopped**

**1 small onion, chopped**

**8 drops Tabasco sauce**

**2 sprigs mint**

**300 ml olive oil**

**croutons for garnish**

**PRAWNS**

**3 dried chillies, chopped**

**2 cloves garlic**

**2 tablespoons oyster sauce**

**1 tablespoon fish sauce**

**3 coriander roots, chopped**

**12 shelled raw prawns**

**JALAPENO SALSA (optional)**

**2 stems coriander**

**1 jalapeno pepper**

**1 tomato, de-seeded**

**½ red onion**

**1 red or green capsicum**

MAKING THE GAZPACHO: Purée all soup ingredients except half the olive oil and the croutons. Pass soup through a coarse sieve. Stir in remaining olive oil. Refrigerate.

COOKING THE PRAWNS: Blend the chillies, garlic, sauces and coriander roots. Fry prawns quickly in this mixture.

MAKING THE SALSA: Finely dice and combine all ingredients.

Spoon soup into bowls and top with chilli prawns. Garnish with salsa and croutons.

**Serves 4**

# Thai Squid Noodles

**SALSA**

**2 tomatoes, diced**

**1 stalk lemon grass, chopped**

**½ red onion, thinly sliced**

**2 spring onions, chopped**

**3 tablespoons chopped coriander**

**2 tablespoons fish sauce**

**1 teaspoon red curry paste**

**1 teaspoon olive oil**

**1 tablespoon red wine vinegar**

**SQUID AND NOODLES**

**3 medium squid tubes**

**olive oil**

**salt**

**ground pepper**

**1 packet thin egg noodles**

MAKING THE SALSA: Mix all the salsa ingredients together. Set aside.

COOKING THE SQUID: Slice side of squid tubes open. Score in a cross-hatch pattern. Slice each tube in half lengthways and each length into three. Coat with small amount of olive oil, and season. Fry in a very hot, lightly oiled pan until squid turns white and tender and curls up (about 2–5 minutes).

Meanwhile blanch noodles in boiling salted water for 2 minutes. Drain.

Mix noodles with salsa and spoon onto a plate or into a bowl. Arrange squid on top and serve.

**Serves 6 as an entrée**

# Roasted Pear and Blue Cheese Salad

**SALAD**

**3 firm ripe pears**

**sunflower oil**

**1 sprig fresh rosemary, crushed**

**salt and pepper**

**1 cup hazelnuts**

**mixed salad leaves**

**200 g or more of your favourite**

**blue cheese**

**fresh herbs, chopped**

**CROUTONS**

**1 x day-old french loaf, sliced**

**thinly for croutons**

**olive oil**

**garlic**

**BALSAMIC VINAIGRETTE**

**olive oil**

**lemon juice**

**balsamic vinegar**

**brown sugar**

**grain mustard**

**salt and ground pepper**

MAKING THE SALAD: Cut pears into eighths, remove cores and lay flat in a baking tin. Drizzle with a little sunflower oil and sprinkle with rosemary, salt and pepper. Toss to coat pears. Roast in a moderate oven until golden and crisp on the edges.

At the same time roast the hazelnuts on a baking tray until skins are dark brown. Cool and rub off skins if desired.

MAKING THE CROUTONS: Lay out bread on baking tray, drizzle with olive oil and rub with garlic. Bake until golden and crisp.

MAKING THE VINAIGRETTE: Combine ingredients to taste.

Toss salad leaves with vinaigrette in a large bowl. Serve piled high onto 4 plates.

Scatter salad with pears, hazelnuts and croutons. Top with thin slices of blue cheese, herbs and croutons.

Salad is also delicious topped with very thin slices of rare roast beef.

**Serves 4**

# Barbecued Lamb with Hummus and Summer Salad

**MARINADE**

½ cup olive oil

4 big cloves garlic

bunch fresh parsley

bunch fresh coriander

zest of 2 lemons or chopped

rind of 1 preserved lemon

(see page 94)

1 small red chilli

1 small onion

**LAMB**

30 lamb cutlets (5 per person)

**HUMMUS**

2 cups chickpeas, soaked

overnight

8 cloves garlic

1 cup olive oil

½ cup lemon juice

salt and ground pepper

2 tablespoons tahini

**SUMMER SALAD**

selection of seasonal vegetables

(courgette, aubergine, red

capsicum, spring onion)

olive oil

salt and ground pepper

tomatoes, chopped

red onion, finely sliced

flat-leaf parsley

lemon juice

**BRUSCHETTA**

1 x day-old french loaf

olive oil

garlic

MAKING THE MARINADE: Mince all marinade ingredients in a food processor.

Marinate cutlets for 8 hours or overnight.

MAKING THE HUMMUS: Boil chickpeas for 1½ hours. Test by flattening one under a thumb. Drain and cool under running water. Purée chickpeas and garlic in a food processor. Add olive oil with motor running and purée into a smooth thick paste. Add lemon juice and seasoning, then tahini. If very thick add a little water to make a creamy consistency.

MAKING THE SALAD: Light the barbecue, slice vegetables into thick slices, drizzle with a little olive oil and season. Grill vegetables then toss with tomatoes, red onion, parsley and lots of lemon juice.

MAKING THE BRUSCHETTA: Slice french loaf diagonally, brush with olive oil and rub with garlic. Barbecue on cooler part of grill.

Barbecue lamb cutlets, basting with marinade.

Place a generous amount of hummus in the centre of each plate and spread slightly. Arrange salad on hummus with lamb on top. Serve with bruschetta.

This can also be made using a selection of winter vegetables.

**Serves 6**

# Dried Fruit Compote with Cardamom Cream

**COMPOTE**

**600 ml dry white wine**

**400 ml water**

**good pinch of saffron strands**

**10 peppercorns  (tied in muslin)**

**1 cinnamon stick**

**50 g sugar**

**150 g dried figs**

**150 g dried apricots**

**150 g pitted prunes**

**scant handful currants**

**CARDAMOM CREAM**

**200 ml cream**

**ground cardamom**

MAKING THE COMPOTE: Bring wine and water to the boil with saffron, peppercorns, cinnamon stick and sugar. Add dried fruits and simmer gently until fruit is tender.

MAKING THE CARDAMOM CREAM: Whip cream until it holds soft peaks and add cardamom to taste.

Serve compote warm or chilled on a flattish plate with fruit mounded in middle, topped with a good dollop of cardamom cream.

Fresh quartered pears may be added halfway through cooking if desired.

**Serves 4**

# Baby Octopus Chargrilled with Ratatouille and Lime Butter

**MARINADE**

**½ cup red wine**

**1 tablespoon honey**

**1 tablespoon olive oil**

**1 tablespoon wholegrain mustard**

**salt and pepper**

**OCTOPUS**

**5 baby octopus per person, beaks and heads removed**

**LIME BUTTER**

**juice and zest of 5 limes**

**250 g butter**

**RATATOUILLE**

**3 tablespoons olive oil**

**1 green zucchini, cut into batons**

**1 yellow zucchini, cut into batons**

**1 red capsicum, thinly sliced**

**1 medium aubergine, sliced**

**fresh oregano and basil**

**salt and pepper**

**10 cherry tomatoes or one large tomato**

**½ cup white wine**

MAKING THE MARINADE: Combine all marinade ingredients.

Blanch octopus for 30 seconds and place in marinade.

MAKING THE LIME BUTTER: Boil lime juice and zest in a saucepan and reduce to about 1 tablespoon. Beat butter until white in colour. Add lime glaze, mix and roll to form a small log. Wrap in foil and refrigerate.

MAKING THE RATATOUILLE: Heat olive oil to sizzling. Add all ingredients except last two. When lightly coloured add tomatoes and wine. Cook for 5 minutes then set aside.

Chargrill octopus until tentacles become crunchy and brown.

Place 2 slices of lime butter on a warm plate. Spoon warm ratatouille over and top with octopus.

**Serves 4**

# Feta Cheese Soufflés with Seared Scallops and Beurre Blanc

**SCALLOPS**

**30 scallops (5 per person)**

**salt and pepper**

**1 tablespoon olive oil**

**SOUFFLÉS**

**25 g butter**

**25 g flour**

**150 ml milk**

**2 egg yolks**

**1 tablespoon freshly grated parmesan**

**125 g feta, chopped**

**fresh nutmeg, grated**

**1½ egg whites**

**6 teaspoons cream**

**extra parmesan for sprinkling**

**2 teaspoons chopped chives**

**BEURRE BLANC**

**½ onion, chopped**

**1 glass dry white wine**

**salt and white pepper**

**1 tablespoon cream**

**250 g unsalted butter, cut into 6 pieces**

PREPARING THE SCALLOPS: Slice off dark thread and wispy fibrous threads. Wash quickly under cold water, drain and place in a bowl. Add seasoning and olive oil. Cover and refrigerate.

MAKING THE SOUFFLÉS: Melt butter in a saucepan, stir in flour and cook over medium heat for 1 minute. Remove from heat for 1 minute then gradually whisk in milk. Return to low heat, whisking constantly until sauce boils and thickens. Remove from heat. Whisk in egg yolks, cheeses, and nutmeg to taste.

Beat egg whites until firm peaks form and fold gently into warm cheese mixture. Spoon into 6 individual buttered soufflé dishes and bake in a water bath at 180°C for about 20 minutes or until well risen and browned. Remove from water bath and set aside to cool to lukewarm. Soufflés will deflate as they cool.

MAKING THE SAUCE: Gently simmer onion and wine. Season and reduce until about 1 tablespoon of liquid is left and onion is moist. Add cream and boil vigorously for 1 minute. Remove saucepan from heat and whisk in 1 piece of butter. Return pan to gentle heat and add remaining butter, 1 piece at a time, each piece being absorbed before next piece added. Do not overheat. Keep sauce in a warm place or in a bain-marie over hot, but not boiling, water.

Place soufflés in an oven dish, pour 1 teaspoon of cream over each one, sprinkle with a little parmesan and place under grill until lightly browned.

Sear scallops until golden in a very hot lightly oiled pan.

Spoon sauce onto hot plates, set soufflé on top and tumble scallops over. Garnish with chives and serve.

**Serves 6**

# Lightly Lemoned Fish with 'Wild' Couscous and Peach Salsa

**WILD COUSCOUS**

**¼ cup wild rice**

**½ medium onion, finely chopped**

**1 clove garlic, crushed**

**1 tablespoon butter**

**1 cup chicken stock**

**1 tablespoon tomato paste**

**¼ teaspoon chopped fresh chilli**

**½ teaspoon turmeric**

**1 teaspoon paprika**

**¾ teaspoon cumin**

**1 tablespoon soy sauce**

**2½ cups couscous**

**½ cup diced red capsicum**

**1 tablespoon finely chopped fresh mint**

**1 tablespoon finely chopped fresh coriander**

**PEACH SALSA**

**¼ cup lime or lemon juice**

**1 cup tomato juice**

**1 tablespoon brown sugar**

**1 tablespoon wholegrain mustard**

**1 teaspoon finely chopped fresh ginger**

**fresh coriander and mint to taste**

**½ cup diced red capsicum**

**¾ cup de-seeded and diced cucumber**

**1 peach per person, stoned, peeled and sliced**

**YOGHURT DRESSING**

**1 cup natural yoghurt**

**1 tablespoon finely chopped fresh mint**

**1 tablespoon finely chopped fresh coriander**

**½ teaspoon cumin**

**salt and pepper**

**FISH**

**4–6 fillets of firm, white fish**

**lemon juice**

**salt and ground pepper**

MAKING THE SALSA: Combine all ingredients and refrigerate to develop flavours.

MAKING THE DRESSING: Combine yoghurt with herbs, cumin and seasoning.

COOKING THE COUSCOUS: Sauté wild rice, onion and garlic in butter. Add chicken stock,

tomato paste, spices and soy
sauce. Simmer and reduce slowly
to a thick paste. Add couscous
and capsicum.

Transfer to a a steamer, steam
for 20 minutes then toss and
steam for a further 10–15
minutes until light and fluffy.
Add mint and coriander.

COOKING THE FISH: Place fish
on a baking tray. Sprinkle with
lemon juice, season and bake
at 180°C until cooked through.

To serve, spoon couscous onto
a plate, arrange fish on top and
spoon yoghurt dressing over.
Arrange salsa on top, allowing
it to spill over and around fish.
Spoon salsa juice around plate.
Serve at once.

**Serves 4–6**

# Mediterranean Chicken Cassoulet

1 raw smoked chicken, portioned, or 1 fresh chicken (do not use cooked smoked chicken – ask your butcher to smoke you one)
100 ml white wine
12 sun-dried tomatoes
2 roasted capsicums, sliced
12 spring onions (white bulbs only)
16 cloves unpeeled garlic, roasted
12 cherry tomatoes
1 tablespoon fresh tarragon leaves
½ litre chicken glaze (reduced chicken stock)

Seal chicken portions in an ovenproof pan. Place in oven at 180°C for 10-15 minutes until cooked through.

Remove chicken from pan, set aside. De-glaze pan with white wine. Add other ingredients to pan and heat through.

Return chicken to pan and reheat.

Serve in large bowls. Accompany with green salad and focaccia.

**Serves 4**

Piccolo

# Macadamia Baklava with Sauterne Peaches

**BAKLAVA**

**1 packet of filo pastry**

**250 g melted butter**

**500 g macadamia nuts, coarsely chopped**

**BAKLAVA SYRUP**

**250 ml water**

**250 g sugar**

**250 ml honey**

**10 cardamom pods**

**½ cinnamon stick**

**POACHING SYRUP**

**500 ml water**

**300 g sugar**

**300 ml sauterne**

**zest of 1 lemon**

**1 cinnamon stick**

**2 cloves**

**1 peach per person, halved and stoned**

MAKING THE BAKLAVA: Make 3 stacks each of 6 sheets of filo. Trim stacks to 15 cm squares.

Layer first 6 filo sheets on a baking tray, brushing each sheet with melted butter.

Spread with a layer of half the macadamia nuts. Layer with another 6 sheets of filo brushed with melted butter. Repeat with another layer of nuts and top with remaining 6 sheets of filo brushed with butter.

Cut carefully into desired portions. Bake at 180°C about 10–15 minutes until golden.

MAKING THE BAKLAVA SYRUP: Boil baklava syrup ingredients to 106°C and remove from heat at soft ball stage, just before it turns to toffee. (Use a sugar thermometer.)

Pour hot syrup over hot baklava. Leave to cool.

MAKING THE POACHING SYRUP: Bring all poaching syrup ingredients except peaches to the boil. Poach peaches in syrup for 5 minutes or until tender. Leave to cool in syrup.

Peel peaches and discard skin. Serve with baklava and thick cream.

**Serves 6–8**

# Eggs en Cocotte with Sorrel and Spinach

**1 tablespoon butter**

**400 g young sorrel and spinach leaves, washed**

**8 eggs**

**salt and pepper to taste**

**8 tablespoons cream**

Melt butter in a frypan. Add sorrel and spinach leaves. Cook over a moderate heat for 3–5 minutes until smooth, then purée.

Divide purée between 4 buttered custard cups. Break 2 eggs into each cup, season and top with 2 tablespoons of cream.

Bake in a bain-marie or water bath for 5–6 minutes at 190°C.

Serve with french bread.

**Serves 4 for breakfast or brunch**

# Baked Rack of Lamb in a Salt and Rosemary Crust

**2 x 250 g racks of lamb**

**1.5 kg rock salt**

**1 large bunch fresh rosemary**

**freshly ground black pepper**

Pre-heat oven to 240°C.

Sprinkle 500 g rock salt and half the rosemary on the bottom of an ovenproof baking dish (preferably a clay dish).

Place racks of lamb on top of the salt and coat completely with the remaining salt, rosemary and ground pepper so that no meat is visible.

Cover dish tightly with foil and bake in oven for 20–25 minutes.

To serve, break off the salt crust and discard. Serve lamb on a plate surrounded with fresh steamed vegetables.

**Serves 2**

# Aubergine and Feta Gratin on Fresh Spinach with Balsamic Syrup

**GRATIN**

**3 large aubergines, cut into slices lengthwise**

**salt**

**olive oil**

**400 g feta cheese**

**1 cup milk**

**ground pepper**

**BALSAMIC SYRUP**

**½ cup balsamic vinegar**

**½ cup maple syrup**

**1 teaspoon arrowroot**

**water**

**400 g fresh spinach leaves, washed**

Preheat oven to 180°C.

MAKING THE GRATIN: Sprinkle unpeeled slices of aubergine with salt and put in a colander for an hour. Rinse and dry slices, brush with olive oil then grill.

Marinate slices of feta cheese in milk, salt and pepper.

In an oven dish alternate layers of aubergine and feta, finishing with a layer of aubergine.

Bake for 10 minutes until feta starts to melt. Take care not to overcook.

MAKING THE BALSAMIC SYRUP: Bring vinegar and maple syrup to the boil. Thicken with arrowroot dissolved in a little water.

Slice gratin into portions. Serve on a bed of spinach leaves. Top with balsamic syrup.

**Serves 6**

## Mondo Mediterranean Salad

**SALAD**

**4 medium courgettes**

**2 red capsicums**

**olive oil**

**salt and ground pepper**

**6 medium tomatoes**

**2 medium red onions**

**16 black olives**

**200 g feta cheese**

**8 large basil leaves**

**TOMATO MARINADE**

**6 cloves garlic, finely chopped**

**½ teaspoon salt**

**1 teaspoon cracked black pepper**

**6 tablespoons balsamic vinegar**

**½ cup olive oil**

**8–10 basil leaves, sliced**

PREPARING THE SALAD: Heat the barbecue. Top and tail courgettes and slice lengthwise about 8 mm thick. Slice capsicums head to tail and remove stem and seeds. Paint both sides of each slice with olive oil and season lightly.

Place courgettes and capsicums on barbecue grill until courgettes are striped brown and capsicums blacken and blister and flesh softens. Set aside to cool.

MAKING THE MARINADE: Whisk together garlic, seasoning and vinegar. Slowly pour in olive oil and continue to whisk. Add basil.

MAKING THE SALAD: Roughly chop tomatoes. Marinate for about 1 hour in marinade.

Slice onions into 2 cm rings. When capsicums have cooled, slice diagonally into strips.

Arrange olives, capsicums, onion, courgettes and tomatoes on a plate. Cumble feta over salad. Spoon tomato marinade over as a dressing.

**Serves 4**

# Barbecued Kingfish on Tomatoes with Smoked Salmon Sour Cream

**TOMATOES**

**700 g beefsteak tomatoes**

**Tomato Marinade (see page 54)**

**SMOKED SALMON SOUR CREAM**

**250 g sour cream**

**1 tablespoon lemon juice**

**½ teaspoon salt**

**½ teaspoon ground pepper**

**180 g smoked salmon offcuts, roughly chopped**

**2 tablespoons roughly chopped dill**

**1 tablespoon roughly chopped mint**

**KINGFISH**

**1 kg kingfish fillets**

**garlic oil (see page 80)**

**salt and pepper**

**1 bunch spring onions, sliced**

**2 lemons, quartered**

Cut tomatoes into thick slices and add to marinade (see page 54 for method).

MAKING THE SMOKED SALMON SOUR CREAM: Mix sour cream with lemon juice and seasoning. Beat with a fork until smooth. Add salmon and herbs. Refrigerate until needed.

COOKING THE FISH: Heat the barbecue. Portion kingfish into 100 g pieces. Paint each piece liberally with garlic oil and season. Barbecue over grill for about 7 minutes each side. Fish should be medium rare, otherwise it will be dry.

Divide tomatoes between 4 plates and arrange kingfish on top. Garnish with smoked salmon sour cream, spring onions and lemon.

**Serves 4**

# Sticky Date Pudding with Butterscotch Sauce

**PUDDING**

**450 ml cold water**

**250 g pitted dates**

**90 g butter**

**250 g caster sugar**

**3 eggs**

**250 g self-raising flour**

**1 heaped teaspoon baking soda**

**1 teaspoon vanilla essence**

**BUTTERSCOTCH SAUCE**

**200 g soft brown sugar**

**½ cup cream**

**100 g butter**

**1 teaspoon vanilla essence**

MAKING THE PUDDING: Pre-heat oven to 180°C. Grease a 260 x 65 mm spring-form cake tin.

Pour cold water over dates and heat slowly in a saucepan.

Meanwhile, cream butter and caster sugar with an electric beater until white. Still beating, add eggs one at a time. Gently add flour.

When dates come to the boil add baking soda and stir until it begins to foam. Add dates and vanilla essence to mixture.

Pour into the cake tin and bake for 40–50 minutes until firm to touch or a skewer comes out with moist crumb.

MAKING THE SAUCE: Combine all sauce ingredients in a saucepan, bring to the boil and simmer for 5 minutes. Pour over top of pudding.

Serve with cream or ice-cream.

**Serves 4**

# Penne with Vegetables, Pesto and Basil Yoghurt

**PENNE**

**1 red onion, diced**

**2 capsicums, sliced and grilled**

**1 x 170 g jar artichoke hearts**

**2 cloves garlic, crushed**

**1 punnet red cherry tomatoes**

**400 g good quality penne pasta**

**200 g basil pesto (bought or home-made)**

**BASIL YOGHURT**

**250 ml natural unsweetened yoghurt**

**3 sprigs of fresh basil, finely chopped**

**1 teaspoon ground black pepper**

**½ fresh chilli, finely diced**

COOKING THE VEGETABLES: Sauté onion, capsicums, artichoke hearts, garlic and cherry tomatoes until onion is translucent.

Cook pasta, drain and add to the pan with vegetables. Add pesto and toss.

MAKING THE BASIL YOGHURT: Combine all dressing ingredients and mix well.

Serve penne hot in large pasta bowls with basil yoghurt drizzled over the top.

**Serves 4**

# Crab Cakes with Coriander and Lemon Remoulade

**CRAB CAKES**

**300 g white fish fillets**

**2 teaspoons ground cumin**

**2 teaspoons ground coriander**

**4 whole chillies**

**4 eggs**

**2 tablespoons cornflour**

**500 g fresh crab meat**

**1 tablespoon butter**

**1 bunch coriander**

**REMOULADE**

**2 cups good-quality mayonnaise**

**1 cup sour cream**

**½ cup finely diced red onion**

**½ cup chopped fresh coriander**

**2 teaspoons lemon zest**

**1 whole chilli, chopped**

MAKING THE CRAB CAKES: Slice fish fillets. Blend on high in food processor with cumin, coriander, chillies, eggs and cornflour. When well combined, fold in crab and leave to stand until ready to use.

MAKING THE REMOULADE: Combine all ingredients and refrigerate until ready to use.

COOKING THE CRAB CAKES: Melt butter in a hot heavy-based frypan. Drop tablespoonsful of crab cake mixture into pan. Turn once bubbles have started to form on top side. Keep cakes hot in oven until ready to serve.

Place crab cakes on a plate, drizzle with remoulade and garnish with fresh coriander.

**Serves 6**

# Chocolate Pâté

**200 g dried apricots**

**200 g pitted prunes**

**½ cup Grand Marnier**

**800 g good quality cooking chocolate**

**200 g butter**

**6 egg yolks**

**100 ml fresh cream**

Chop apricots and prunes and marinate in Grand Marnier for at least one hour.

Melt chocolate and butter in a double boiler. When melted, stir in egg yolks one at a time. Thin mixture with the cream and set aside to cool.

When cool, combine all ingredients well and pour into a lightly greased loaf tin. Refrigerate or or freeze.

Turn pâté out onto a plate. Slice with a hot knife. Serve with fresh fruit.

Pâté can be made 2–3 days in advance.

**Serves up to 12**

# Chicken Mulawa with Raita

**CHICKEN**

**6 boned chicken fillets, skinned**

**750 ml thick natural yoghurt**

**2 tablespoons tandoori masala**

**1 tablespoon ground coriander**

**1 tablespoon ground cumin**

**1 teaspoon salt**

**4 large cloves garlic**

**small piece of fresh ginger**

**2 onions, finely diced**

**1 tablespoon butter**

**50 ml tomato paste**

**200 ml fresh cream**

**bunch of fresh coriander,
chopped**

**RAITA**

**1 cup acidophilus yoghurt**

**½ onion, finely diced**

**⅓ cup diced cucumber**

**fresh mint, finely chopped**

**juice of 1 lemon**

**salt to taste**

MARINATING THE CHICKEN:
Slice chicken into long thin strips
and marinate for at least 1 hour
in yoghurt, tandoori masala,
coriander, cumin and salt.

Crush garlic and finely slice
ginger. Crush both of these
together until they form a paste.

COOKING THE CHICKEN: Sauté
onions in butter until translucent.
Add garlic and ginger paste.
Slowly add tomato paste. Cook
gently until all ingredients are
well combined.

Add chicken and all the
marinade. Cook over a medium
heat until chicken is cooked.

MAKING THE RAITA: Mix all
raita ingredients and refrigerate
for 1 hour.

Just before serving add fresh
cream and coriander. (This dish
can be made the day before and
cream added when reheating.)

Serve chicken and raita with
basmati rice, poppadoms and
sliced bananas.

**Serves 6**

# Strawberries with Fine Sable Biscuits and Lemon Mascarpone

**BISCUITS**

**75 g soft unsalted butter**

**100 g plain flour, sifted**

**40 g caster sugar**

**½ teaspoon finely grated lemon zest**

**2 egg yolks**

**MASCARPONE MIX**

**300 g mascarpone**

**juice and zest of 1 lemon**

**icing sugar to taste**

**COULIS**

**750 g strawberries**

**50 ml Grand Marnier**

**icing sugar to taste**

MAKING THE BISCUITS: Rub butter into flour, sugar and zest until mixture resembles breadcrumbs. Add egg yolks. Combine well, cover dough and refrigerate.

When cold, roll out very thin and cut 8 biscuits with a fluted 8 cm cutter.

Place on a greased or non-stick baking tray. Bake in pre-heated oven at 200°C for 8 minutes or until lightly brown. Cool.

MAKING THE MASCARPONE MIX: Combine ingredients in a bowl and refrigerate.

MAKING THE COULIS: Hull a third of the strawberries and purée in food processor with a little icing sugar and Grand Marnier. Taste. Add more icing sugar if necessary. Pass mixture through a sieve and set coulis aside.

Hull and cut remaining strawberries in half.

Spoon a small amount of coulis onto centre of each plate. Place 1 biscuit on top and spread a spoonful of mascarpone mixture over. Top with strawberries and another biscuit. Dust top biscuit with icing sugar and top with a strawberry.

**Serves 4**

# Zing Malaysian Fish Curry

30 g fresh tamarind

250 ml water

1 medium to large onion, finely chopped

1 tablespoon crushed ginger

1 tablespoon crushed garlic

1 tablespoon Belcan shrimp paste

50 ml vegetable oil

1 heaped tablespoon cumin seed

3 tablespoons fish curry powder

1½ teaspoons ground paprika

400 ml coconut cream

200 ml milk

200 ml natural unsweetened yoghurt

salt and pepper to taste

fresh coriander leaves

800 g fresh skinned and boned terakihi fillets

2 large firm tomatoes, quartered

Bring tamarind and water to the boil in a small saucepan. At a rolling simmer reduce by half. Allow tamarind to soften and water to turn the colour of tea, about 20-25 minutes. Remove from heat and strain. Set juice aside and discard solids.

Sauté onion, ginger, garlic and shrimp paste in oil until onion is almost transparent. Add cumin seed and sauté 3 minutes. Reduce heat, add fish curry powder and paprika, stirring constantly, and sauté until fragrant.

Add coconut cream, milk, yoghurt and tamarind juice, stirring as mixture comes to the boil. Reduce heat. Simmer for 10 minutes to thicken, taking care not to over-thicken as this mixture will be used to poach the fish. Season to taste. Cover sauce and refrigerate, preferably overnight, to infuse flavours.

Pour curry sauce into a large
pan and bring to the boil. If too
thick, thin with a little milk or
cream. Reduce heat. Lay fish
fillets flat in pan, covering with
sauce. Allow fish to poach
for 8–10 minutes. Add tomato
wedges and poach for 3 minutes.

Place cooked fish on plates.
Ladle curry sauce over. Arrange
tomato on top. Garnish with
fresh coriander leaves and serve
with coconut and lemon grass
steamed rice (see page 72).

**Serves 4**

# Coconut and Lemon Grass-steamed Rice

**2 cups long-grain rice, washed**

**100 ml coconut cream**

**900 ml water**

**1 bulb fresh lemon grass**

**salt to taste**

In a small saucepan allow rice, coconut cream, water, lemon grass and salt to come to the boil on low to medium heat. Remove from heat.

Place a clean dry cotton teatowel over top of the saucepan and place a heavy skillet on top. This will seal the steam inside the pot and steam the rice. Leave rice for 20–25 minutes.

Wet the inside of a teacup. Pack rice quickly (to avoid water absorption) and firmly into the cup. Invert cup over serving plate. Tap edge of cup firmly to release moulded rice onto plate.

**Serves 4**

# Tiger Prawns and Stir-fried Vegetables on Grilled Polenta

**POLENTA**

**750 ml chicken stock**

**½ medium onion, finely chopped**

**1 teaspoon chopped fresh basil**

**1 teaspoon chopped fresh oregano**

**1 bay leaf**

**100 g polenta**

**salt and ground pepper**

**100 g unsalted butter**

**1 tomato, sliced**

**½ cup grated cheese**

**PRAWNS**

**salt and ground pepper**

**16 unshelled tiger prawns**

**melted butter**

**VEGETABLES**

**salt and pepper**

**4 slices aubergine, 1 cm thick**

**4 teaspoons olive oil**

**1 teaspoon finely chopped garlic**

**1 teaspoon finely chopped ginger**

**1 large field mushroom, sliced into long strips**

**1 large courgette, cut into long batons**

**½ medium-sized red capsicum, cut into long strips**

**½ medium-sized yellow capsicum, cut into long strips**

**white wine**

**soy sauce**

**4 balls bocconcini marinated in flavoured oil, salt and herbs**

COOKING THE POLENTA: Bring chicken stock to the boil with onion, basil, oregano and bay leaf. Add polenta slowly in a steady stream, stirring all the time until a thick porridge-like consistency is reached. (Add more polenta if necessary.)

Remove from heat, season and add butter. Stir to combine. Pour mixture into small round tart tin or dish. Cover with tomato and cheese. Bake at 180°C until brown, about 15–20 minutes. Remove and allow to cool.

COOKING THE PRAWNS: season prawns and brush with a little melted butter. Bake in 200°C oven for 5–6 minutes or until colour changes.

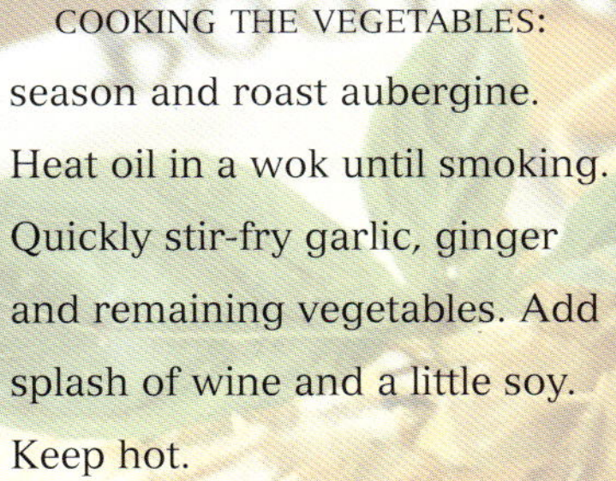

COOKING THE VEGETABLES: season and roast aubergine. Heat oil in a wok until smoking. Quickly stir-fry garlic, ginger and remaining vegetables. Add splash of wine and a little soy. Keep hot.

Slice bocconcini into thick slices.

Cut polenta into 4 wedges. Place under a hot grill for 3 minutes until heated through.

Place a polenta wedge in the centre of a heated plate. Pile vegetables on top as high as possible. Top with artistically arranged prawns, aubergine and bocconcini. Serve at once.

**Serves 4**

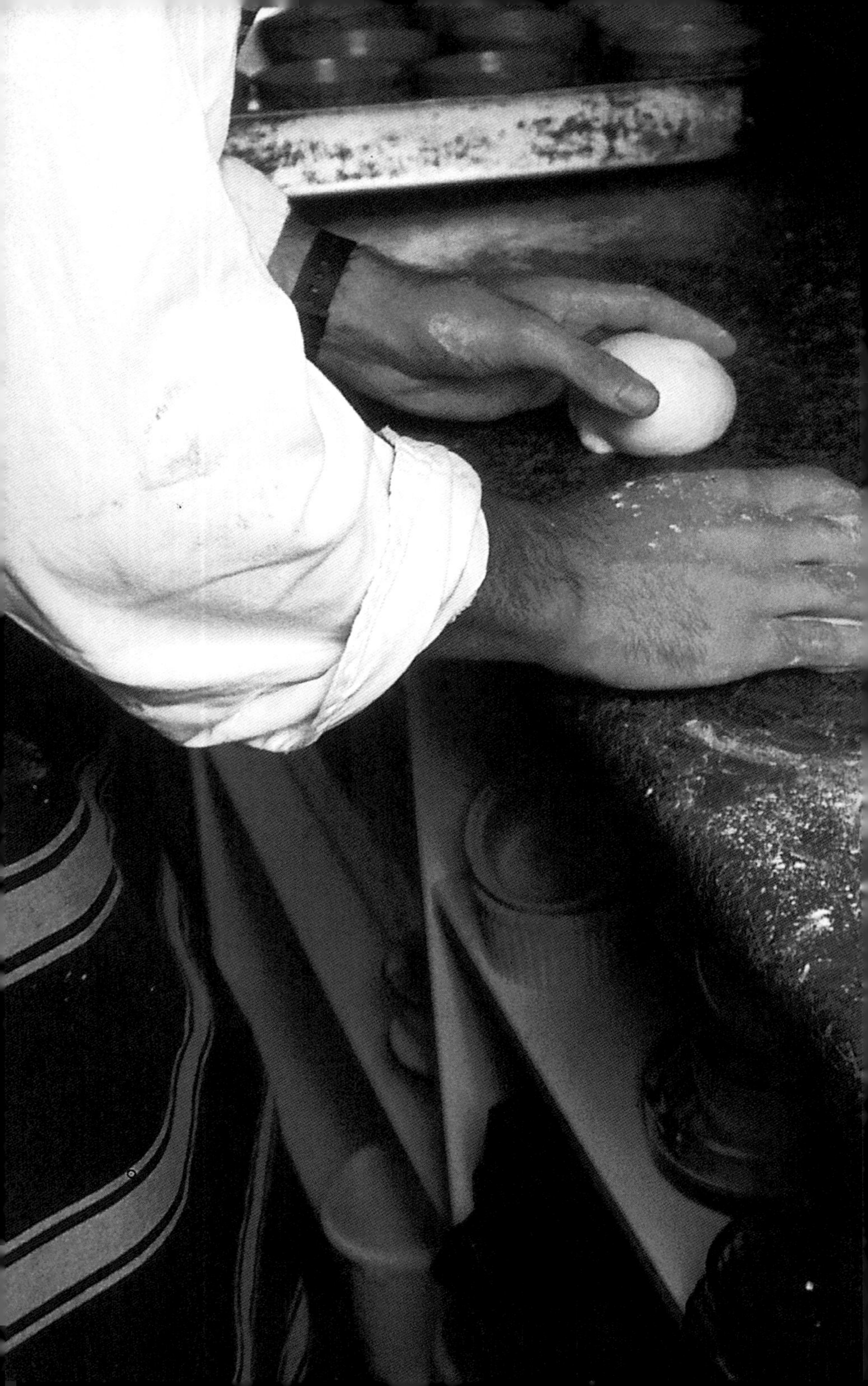

# Seafood Ragout

100 g unsalted butter

1 cup finely diced onion

garlic

1 tablespoon chopped ginger

1 tablespoon minced lemon grass

white wine

400 ml coconut cream

12 medium cockles in shells, cleaned

8 green lip mussels in shells, de-bearded

150 g calamari, cut into rings

400 g white fish fillets, cut into 2 cm cubes

4 crab claws

1 tablespoon good green curry paste

1 tablespoon coriander and walnut pesto (if unavailable use fresh coriander)

1 tablespoon lemon juice

salt and pepper

16 large scallops

200 g salmon fillet, boned and cubed

200 g cooked jasmine rice

fresh herbs for garnish

tomato concasse for garnish

In a large heavy skillet heat butter until foaming. Add onions, garlic, ginger and lemon grass. Sweat over high heat about 2 minutes until soft.

Deglaze the pan with a splash of white wine, add coconut cream and all ingredients except scallops, salmon and rice. Cover and simmer for 2-3 minutes. Add scallops and salmon. Turn up heat and reduce for 1 minute.

Divide hot rice between 4 heated bowls. Spoon seafood attractively on top and spoon sauce over. Garnish with fresh herbs and tomato concasse.

**Serves 4**

# Feta and Spinach Crostini with Rosemary Pepper Honey

**GARLIC OIL**

**100 ml olive oil**

**3 cloves garlic**

**ROSEMARY PEPPER HONEY**

**½ cup clear liquid honey**

**¼ cup water**

**2 teaspoons chopped fresh rosemary**

**1 teaspoon cracked black pepper**

**CROSTINI**

**1 french loaf**

**12 medium spinach leaves, washed**

**150 g feta cheese**

**½ red capsicum, thinly sliced**

MAKING THE GARLIC OIL: chop garlic and add to oil. Pour into a glass jar with a tight lid. Leave to infuse for about 1 week.

MAKING THE ROSEMARY PEPPER HONEY: In a small saucepan combine the honey, water, rosemary and pepper. Simmer, swirling pan occasionally, until mix is reduced to about half a cup. Cool honey to room temperature, pour into a glass jar and seal tightly.

MAKING THE CROSTINI: Slice french bread diagonally 1 cm thick. Brush with garlic oil and toast in oven until lightly golden.

Blanch spinach leaves briefly in boiling water. Refresh under cold water and drain.

Lay one spinach leaf on each slice of bread. Cut feta into ½ cm slices and place slice on top of spinach. Top with a few strips of capsicum and drizzle with garlic oil. Bake 5 minutes in moderate oven.

To serve, arrange 3 crostini per person on a serving plate.

Spoon 3 tablespoons or so of the rosemary pepper honey over each serving of crostini. Garnish with spinach leaves and feta.

**Serves 4**

# Warm Chicken Salad with Orange and Yoghurt Dressing

**DRESSING**

**500 ml plain unsweetened yoghurt**

**½ teaspoon caster sugar**

**6 drops Tabasco sauce**

**salt and pepper to taste**

**150 ml fresh orange juice**

**SALAD**

**2 teaspoons oil**

**4 chicken fillets**

**mixed salad greens**

**orange segments**

**2 teaspoons pine nuts**

**cracked pepper**

**fresh herbs**

MAKING THE DRESSING: Mix all dressing ingredients together. Refrigerate.

MAKING THE SALAD: Heat oil in a frypan and fry chicken until golden.

Arrange chicken on salad greens with orange segments and pine nuts. Drizzle with dressing. Sprinkle with a little cracked pepper and fresh herbs.

**Serves 4**

# Salmon Steaks with Tomato Salsa on Chilli Grits

**SALSA**

**½ cup sun-dried tomatoes, finely chopped**

**200 g wild mushrooms (or oyster or shiitake), roasted and finely chopped**

**¼ teaspoon salt**

**¼ teaspoon ground pepper**

**6 tablespoons olive oil**

**¼ small onion, finely chopped**

**4 tablespoons balsamic vinegar**

**½ teaspoon brown sugar**

**1 tablespoon finely chopped fresh coriander**

**pinch of chilli powder**

**1 teaspoon dry white wine**

**CHILLI GRITS**

**1 cup cream**

**2 shallots or ¼ onion, finely diced**

**1 clove garlic, finely diced**

**½ cup grits (polenta)**

**1 teaspoon finely chopped fresh coriander**

**1 green chilli (or more)**

**¼ cup water**

**salt and pepper to taste**

**SALMON**

**4 salmon steaks**

**oil**

**fresh herbs**

MAKING THE SALSA: Mix all salsa ingredients together. Refrigerate.

MAKING THE GRITS: Simmer cream, shallots, garlic and grits in a heavy saucepan for about 10 minutes, stirring occasionally.

Blend coriander, chilli and water in blender until smooth. Add to grits and simmer for about 7 minutes. Grits should be sloppy.

Remove from heat and season to taste. Use immediately or re-heat in microwave when needed.

COOKING THE SALMON: Fry salmon steaks in a hot, lightly oiled frypan for 3–4 minutes on both sides until golden and just cooked in middle.

Spoon hot grits into the centre of a large platter. Place salmon on top and cover with salsa. Garnish with fresh herbs.

**Serves 4**

# Millefeuille of Scallops with Relish and Lime and Chive Beurre Blanc

**PASTRY**

**1 packet pre-rolled puff pastry sheets**

**1 egg, beaten**

**RELISH**

**10 g dried red capsicum**

**500 g whole-kernel corn**

**150 ml white wine vinegar**

**50 ml water**

**150 g sugar**

**1 teaspoon turmeric**

**1 teaspoon ground cumin**

**½ teaspoon ground star anise**

**½ onion, finely chopped**

**BEURRE BLANC**

**¼ cup white wine**

**1 tablespoon white wine vinegar**

**3 tablespoons cream**

**100 g diced butter**

**juice of ½ lime**

**1 tablespoon chopped chives**

**SCALLOPS**

**3 dozen scallops**

**clarified butter**

**2 limes cut into wedges**

**extra chives for garnish**

PREPARING THE PASTRY: Cut pastry into 18 triangles (about 10 cm each along base). Set on a baking tray and brush with beaten egg. Bake 10-15 minutes at 210°C until golden brown.

MAKING THE RELISH: Combine all relish ingredients in a pot and simmer until a thick consistency.

MAKING THE BEURRE BLANC: Reduce wine and vinegar to a syrupy consistency, add cream and reduce again until thick. Remove from heat and whisk in butter a few cubes at a time. Add lime juice and chives.

COOKING THE SCALLOPS: Sauté scallops in clarified butter in a hot pan.

Spoon some relish in centre of plates, top with 1 pastry triangle. Cover with relish, 3 scallops, beurre blanc and chives. Repeat layers, finishing with pastry. Garnish with lime wedges and chives.

**Serves 6**

# Chargrilled Salmon Steak with Rouille, Vinaigrette and Gremolata

**ROUILLE**

**2 red capsicums**

**1 fresh red chilli**

**4 cloves garlic**

**1 teaspoon salt**

**black pepper to taste**

**squeeze of lemon juice**

**2 egg yolks**

**1½ cups olive oil**

**YELLOW PEPPER VINAIGRETTE**

**2 yellow capsicums, roasted and peeled**

**⅓ cup white wine vinegar**

**1 cup oil**

**salt and pepper**

**1 teaspoon sugar**

**GREMOLATA**

**100 g parsley**

**zest of 5 lemons**

**8 cloves garlic, finely chopped**

**SALMON**

**6 salmon steaks**

**lemon wedges**

MAKING THE ROUILLE: De-seed and de-vein capsicums and chilli. Brush with olive oil and roast. Remove the skins.

In a food processor blend capsicums, chilli, garlic, salt, pepper and lemon juice. With motor running, add egg yolks one at a time. Slowly add oil to form mayonnaise.

MAKING THE VINAIGRETTE: Blend capsicums, add other vinaigrette ingredients and blend again.

MAKING THE GREMOLATA: Blend parsley, lemon zest and garlic.

COOKING THE SALMON: Chargrill salmon steaks until just done.

Cover steaks with rouille, drizzle with vinaigrette and top with gremolata. Garnish with lemon wedges.

**Serves 6**

# Lavender-steeped Crème Brûlée with Sugar Shards and Langues de Chat

**BRÛLÉE**

**¼ cup caster sugar**

**6 egg yolks**

**1 teaspoon vanilla essence**

**125-150 g lavender flowers, leaves and stalks**

**600 ml cream**

**4 tablespoons caster sugar**

**6 strawberries (optional) for garnish**

**extra lavender flowers for garnish**

**LANGUES DE CHAT**

**65 g butter**

**65 g icing sugar**

**1–2 drops vanilla essence**

**65 g flour**

**1 flat tsp cornflour**

**1½ egg whites**

**SUGAR SHARDS**

**110 g caster sugar**

**55 ml water**

**25 ml glucose**

MAKING THE BRÛLÉE: Cream sugar and egg yolks with vanilla essence.

Simmer lavender in cream, crushing flowers occasionally to extract flavour. Strain cream and pour onto sugar and egg mix. Stir constantly over low heat until mixture coats the back of a wooden spoon.

Pour into 6 ramekins of 8 cm diameter. Bake in a water bath or bain-marie at 150°C for 1 hour. Allow to cool.

Sprinkle top of brûlée with caster sugar and caramelise under hot grill.

MAKING THE LANGUES DE CHAT: Cream together butter, icing sugar and vanilla.

Sift flour and cornflour together and add to creamed ingredients. Beat in egg whites, a little at a time.

Pipe into traditional 'cat's tongue' shape, about 6 cm long (or as desired) on a greased tray.

Bake at 205°C until pale golden brown.

MAKING THE SUGAR SHARDS: Combine shard ingredients in a stainless steel saucepan. Simmer gently until a golden brown.

Pour carefully onto a large baking tray and allow mixture to spread over the tray. Cool and break sheet into shards.

Place a ramekin of créme brûlée onto each plate. Stab shards into brûlée decoratively. Garnish with a strawberry and lavender flowers. Place langue de chat around plate.

**Serves 6**

# Baked Goat's Cheese with Lemon Herb Vinaigrette

**MARINADE**

**1 cup olive oil**

**fresh sprig rosemary, oregano and thyme**

**6 peppercorns**

**6 coriander seeds, crushed**

**CHEESE**

**660 g goat's cheese (Kapiti Chèvre if available), cut into serving slices**

**2 cups fresh breadcrumbs**

**finely chopped herbs (e.g. parsley or chives)**

**salt and ground pepper**

**mesclun (mixed baby salad leaves)**

**VINAIGRETTE**

**lemon juice**

**olive oil**

**salt and ground pepper**

MARINATING THE CHEESE: Warm marinade ingredients. Cool and add cheese. (Cheese can be marinated well in advance, preferably at least a week ahead, and stored in a preserving jar. Leftover cheese will keep in marinade for 6 months or longer.)

Remove cheese from marinade.

Mix breadcrumbs with herbs and seasoning. Roll cheese in breadcrumbs.

Place on baking tray and bake at 180°C for 5 minutes or until cheese is soft.

MAKING THE VINAIGRETTE: Mix ingredients to taste.

Toss mesclun lightly with vinaigrette and serve with hot baked cheese on top.

**Serves 6 as an entrée**

# Warm Provençale Chickpea Salad

**CHICKPEA SALAD**

**2 cups chickpeas, soaked overnight**

**salt**

**2 large onions**

**¼ cup olive oil**

**1 tablespoon chopped garlic**

**2 teaspoons fresh oregano**

**selection of fresh vegetables (aubergine, capsicum, carrot, pumpkin, courgette, french beans)**

**200 g feta cheese**

**MARINADE**

**1 tablespoon cumin seed, toasted then ground**

**½ cup lemon juice**

**2 teaspoons salt**

**1 teaspoon freshly ground pepper**

**pinch cayenne pepper**

**1 cup kalamata olives, pitted and chopped**

**PRESERVED LEMON PEEL**

**lemons**

**salt**

**cloves**

**coriander seeds**

**bay leaves**

**extra lemon juice**

MAKING THE SALAD: Boil chickpeas until tender in plenty of water. Add salt during last 10 minutes. Drain.

Cut onion into 1 cm rings. Sauté in olive oil with garlic and oregano.

MAKING THE MARINADE: Combine marinade ingredients.

Add marinade to chickpeas and onions. Set aside for one hour or longer.

Cut vegetables into wedges. Grill, roast or steam.

PRESERVING THE LEMON PEEL: Scrub lemons and soak in cold water for 3 days, changing water daily. Cut lemons into quarters or smaller.

Place a spoonful of salt into a 1½-litre sterilised jar and layer lemons with more salt, cloves, coriander seeds and bay leaves until jar is full of lemons (about

18 lemons). Pack down tightly. Completely cover with extra lemon juice and salt. Seal and leave for 1 month before using. (Will keep for a year or more.) To use, discard lemon pulp and slice the peel thinly.

Combine chickpeas and hot vegetables. Garnish with feta and preserved lemon peel if desired.

**Serves 12 as an entrée
or 6 as a main course**

# Basbousa (Middle Eastern Semolina Cake)

**SYRUP**

**2 cups sugar**

**½ cup water**

**1 tablespoon lemon juice**

**1 dessertspoon honey**

**CAKE**

**155 g butter**

**1 cup caster sugar**

**½ teaspoon vanilla**

**4 eggs**

**2½ cups semolina**

**1¼ teaspoons baking powder**

**¾ teaspoon baking soda**

**1 cup natural yoghurt**

**⅓ cup coarsely chopped almonds**

MAKING THE SYRUP: Bring sugar, water and lemon juice to the boil. Simmer for 10 minutes. Add honey. Cool.

MAKING THE CAKE: Cream butter, caster sugar and vanilla. Add eggs one at a time.

Sift dry ingredients twice and fold in alternately with yoghurt, starting and ending with dry ingredients.

Spread into greased 20 x 30 cm baking dish and sprinkle with chopped almonds. Bake at 180°C for 25–30 minutes.

Pour cool syrup over hot cake. Serve with thickened yoghurt. (Hang yoghurt in muslin over a bowl for a couple of hours. Excess liquid will drip out.)

**Serves 12**

# Lamb Fillets on Chargrilled Vegetable Risotto with Roasted Capsicum Vinaigrette

**RISOTTO**

1 medium aubergine

2 large courgettes

salt

½ cup olive oil

juice and zest of 1 lemon

1 cup shredded basil leaves

2 cloves garlic, minced

1 medium red capsicum

½ onion, diced

4 tablespoons butter

1 cup arborio rice

4 cups warm chicken stock

**VINAIGRETTE**

1 small red capsicum

½ cup wine vinegar

1½ cups olive oil

salt to taste

**LAMB**

12 lean lamb fillets

MAKING THE RISOTTO: Cut aubergine into slices and courgettes into strips. Place in a bowl, sprinkle liberally with salt, and cover and stand for at least 30 minutes to draw out juices. Drain and pat dry with a teatowel. Brush with olive oil and chargrill or roast in a hot oven until soft.

While warm, dress with ½ cup of olive oil, lemon juice and zest, basil and garlic. Cover.

Roast capsicum in hot oven until skin blisters. Remove and place in tightly sealed plastic bag. When cooled, peel and remove seeds. Chop roughly and combine with other vegetables.

In a large heavy frypan lightly sauté onion in melted butter over medium to high heat.

Add rice and sauté until opaque and evenly coated with butter. Reduce heat and slowly add 1 cup of stock.

Stir constantly until liquid is absorbed then add another ½ cup of stock. Continue adding stock, stirring constantly, until rice is al dente.

Add chargrilled vegetables in their dressing with enough remaining stock to make risotto moist, not sloppy.

MAKING THE VINAIGRETTE: Prepare capsicum as for risotto and blend with salt and vinegar in a food processor. With motor running slowly incorporate oil.

Sear lamb fillets on all sides in a hot frypan. Remove and slice lamb diagonally against the grain.

Serve on mound of risotto surrounded by vinaigrette.

**Serves 4**

# Roasted Pumpkin Gnocchi with Pesto Cream Sauce

**GNOCCHI**

**200 g skinned pumpkin, roasted**

**1 egg yolk**

**1 tablespoon garlic oil**

**(see page 80)**

**salt and pepper**

**50 g plain flour**

**PESTO CREAM SAUCE**

**150 g basil**

**½ cup garlic oil**

**1½ cups white wine**

**1 cup cream**

**salt and pepper to taste**

**parmesan cheese**

MAKING THE GNOCCHI: Purée pumpkin, egg, garlic oil and seasoning.

Using a wooden spoon lightly fold the flour into the pumpkin purée. (Dough should form a ball leaving the sides of the bowl clean.)

Bring a large pot of water to the boil. Break off pieces of dough (about golf-ball size) and place in water. Simmer gnocchi until they float to the surface of the water. Remove with a slotted spoon.

MAKING THE SAUCE: Blend basil in a food processor. With the motor running slowly add oil until a thick paste is formed. In a frypan reduce white wine over a high heat to about 50 ml. Stir in basil pesto and add cream. Season and add parmesan. Reduce by one-third.

Top gnocchi with cream sauce and grated parmesan. Place under a hot grill until lightly browned.

**Serves 4 as an entrée**

# THE CAFES

**Anatole's Cafe**
The County Hotel, 12 Browning Street, Napier. (06) 835 7800

**Andiamo**
194 Jervois Road, Herne Bay, Auckland. (09) 378 7811

**Boat Shed Cafe**
350 Wakefield Quay, Nelson. (03) 546 9783

**Cafe Paradiso**
20 Courtney Place, Wellington. (04) 384 3887

**City Bistro and Bar**
Civic Square, Harris Street entrance, Wellington. (04) 801 8828

**Coyote Street Bar and Restaurant**
126 Oxford Terrace, Christchurch. (03) 366 6055

**The Garnet Road Foodstore**
162 Garnet Road, Westmere, Auckland. (09) 376 8227

**The Lido Cafe**
Corner Wakefield and Victoria Streets, Wellington. (04) 499 6666

**Mondo Cucina**
15 Blair Street, Wellington. (04) 801 6615

**Ombrellos Caffè**
10 Clarendon Street, Dunedin. (03) 477 8773

**Piccolo's Restaurant**
Corner Lyndon Road and Nelson Street, Hastings. (06) 878 1188

**Safran**
71 Davis Crescent, Newmarket, Auckland. (09) 520 5664

**Solera Vino**
25 Beach Street, Queenstown. (03) 442 9585

**Stella**
118 Ponsonby Road, Ponsonby, Auckland. (09) 378 7979

**Sumner's Wine Bar and Restaurant**
29 Wakefield Avenue, Christchurch. (03) 326 7230

**Zing Cafe**
Corner Wakefield and Blair Streets, Wellington. (04) 385 0111

# INDEX

VIKING

Penguin Books (NZ) Ltd, 182-190 Wairau Road, Auckland 10, New Zealand
Penguin Books Ltd, 27 Wrights Lane, London W8 5TZ, England
Penguin USA, 375 Hudson Street, New York, NY 10014, United States
Penguin Books Australia Ltd, 487 Maroondah Highway, Ringwood, Australia 3134
Penguin Books Canada Ltd, 10 Alcorn Avenue, Toronto, Ontario, Canada M4V 3B2

Penguin Books Ltd, Registered Offices:  Harmondsworth, Middlesex, England

First published by Penguin Books (New Zealand) Ltd in 1996
10  9  8  7  6  5  4  3  2  1

This selection and Introduction © Penguin Books (NZ) Ltd, 1996

Individual recipes in this book © respective cafes as per contents page



Typesetting by Claire O'Connor Graphic Studio
Printed in Singapore
ISBN 0-670.87186.9